Alberta D. Jones

LIKE A DRAGON
YAKUZA IN HAWAII

GAME GUIDE

Sail, Fight, and Conquer

Chapter 1: Introduction to Like a Dragon: Pirate Yakuza in Hawaii

1.1 Overview of the Game

A New Chapter in the Like a Dragon Series

Like a Dragon: Pirate Yakuza in Hawaii is an ambitious spin-off in the renowned *Like a Dragon* (formerly *Yakuza*) franchise. Developed by **Ryu Ga Gotoku Studio** and published by **Sega**, this installment takes the series in an entirely new direction, blending its signature over-the-top action and gripping storytelling with a high-seas pirate adventure.

Departing from the neon-lit streets of Kamurocho and Ijincho, players are thrust into the **tropical waters of Hawaii and its surrounding islands**, where crime, treasure, and mystery await. While previous entries focused on modern Japanese crime syndicates, this game introduces **a swashbuckling world of outlaws, rogue pirate factions, and maritime conflict**, all while retaining the series' signature humor, drama, and thrilling combat.

The Story: Majima's New Adventure

At the heart of the game is **Goro Majima**, the unpredictable and beloved "Mad Dog of Shimano." Unlike past protagonists, Majima is not in his familiar Yakuza setting—he awakens **shipwrecked on a mysterious island off the coast of Hawaii**, with no recollection of how he got there.

As he navigates this unfamiliar land, Majima soon finds himself entangled with **Hawaiian pirate crews, corrupt crime lords, and treasure-seeking outlaws**. With danger lurking at every turn, he must build his own crew, reclaim his lost memories, and uncover a legendary hidden treasure rumored to be buried deep in the islands.

The narrative is filled with **classic Yakuza-style emotional depth, unexpected betrayals, and larger-than-life characters**, keeping players hooked from start to finish.

Gameplay Innovations: A Pirate's Life Meets Yakuza Combat

While the game retains the **signature beat 'em up combat system**, it introduces several **new mechanics** that reflect its pirate theme:

- **Dual Combat Styles**: Players can switch between two fighting styles—
    - **Mad Dog Style** (fast-paced, acrobatic, dual-wielding combat)
    - **Sea Dog Style** (uses cutlasses, pistols, and pirate-themed weapons)
- **Naval Exploration**: Players can **sail between islands** on Majima's personal ship, the **Goromaru**, encountering **random events, enemy pirate ships, and hidden treasures.**
- **Ship Battles**: Real-time naval combat allows players to **fire cannons, board enemy vessels, and engage in ship deck brawls.**
- **Open-World Island Exploration**: Players can visit **Honolulu, Rich Island, Madlantis, and other hidden locations**, each filled with **side quests, secret bosses, and mini-games.**

Classic Yakuza Elements Remain

Despite the fresh pirate setting, the game **retains what fans love about the series**:

- **Side Quests**: Expect bizarre, hilarious, and heartwarming encounters with **quirky NPCs.**
- **Mini-Games**: Karaoke, gambling, fishing, and even a **new "Island Survival" mini-game** where players gather resources and craft pirate gear.
- **Dramatic Storytelling**: The game expertly balances **serious crime drama** with over-the-top, laugh-out-loud moments.

1.2 Story Premise: Majima's Pirate Odyssey

A Mad Dog Lost at Sea

In *Like a Dragon: Pirate Yakuza in Hawaii*, the spotlight shifts to **Goro Majima**, the enigmatic and unpredictable "Mad Dog of Shimano." Known for his wild personality, razor-sharp wit, and chaotic fighting style, Majima has always been a fan favorite in the *Like a Dragon* series. However, this time, he's far from the familiar neon-soaked streets of Kamurocho, thrust into an entirely new environment where his survival instincts are tested like never before.

The story begins with **Majima awakening on the shores of a remote island near Hawaii**, battered, bruised, and—most importantly—without any memory of how he got there. His iconic eyepatch, snake-skin jacket, and sharp blades are all that remain of his former life. Stripped of his past, Majima must navigate a world teeming with pirates, smugglers, and criminals, all while piecing together fragments of his forgotten memories.

The Journey for Identity and Treasure

As Majima regains his footing in this strange land, he discovers that the island isn't just any tropical paradise—**it's part of a larger archipelago riddled with pirate factions, hidden treasures, and dark conspiracies.** Despite having no recollection of his past, his natural charisma and ferocity quickly earn him the respect (and fear) of those around him.

Before long, Majima becomes the unlikely **captain of a ragtag pirate crew**, aboard his ship, the **Goromaru**. His mission? To **find a legendary treasure hidden somewhere within the Hawaiian islands**, a prize that could hold the key to unlocking both unimaginable wealth and the secrets of his lost past. But this is no simple treasure hunt—**Majima's journey is tangled in a web of betrayal, ancient curses, and ruthless enemies** who would kill to claim the prize for themselves.

The World of Pirates and Criminal Syndicates

Hawaii in this universe is far from a serene tourist destination. It's a melting pot of cultures, crime, and chaos, where **pirate factions rule the seas**, and **crime syndicates control the land**. Majima will have to navigate both worlds, dealing with:

- **Rival Pirate Captains:** Ruthless seafarers who will stop at nothing to seize control of the islands and the ocean's treasures.
- **Corrupt Crime Lords:** Yakuza-like figures embedded within Honolulu's underworld, pulling strings behind the scenes.

- **Rebels and Outcasts:** Unlikely allies who may aid or betray Majima, depending on the choices he makes.

Each encounter pushes Majima closer to the truth about his past and the real reason he was brought to these cursed waters.

Themes of Redemption, Loyalty, and Chaos

At its core, *Pirate Yakuza in Hawaii* isn't just about treasure and pirate battles—it's a story about **identity, redemption, and loyalty**. Majima, despite being known for his chaotic nature, is a character deeply rooted in loyalty and honor. This journey forces him to question:

- **Who is he without his Yakuza past?**
- **Can he trust the crew he's assembled, or will betrayal strike from within?**
- **Is the treasure he seeks material wealth, or is it something far more personal—like the missing pieces of his soul?**

As players guide Majima through stormy seas and treacherous alliances, they'll experience an emotional odyssey filled with **epic battles, heart-wrenching decisions, and moments of outrageous Yakuza-style humor.**

1.3 Key Features and What's New

Like a Dragon: Pirate Yakuza in Hawaii marks a bold evolution in the *Like a Dragon* series, introducing fresh mechanics, new environments, and gameplay innovations while maintaining the franchise's signature charm. This spin-off combines the gritty, character-driven storytelling of the Yakuza universe with thrilling pirate adventures, naval warfare, and tropical exploration. Here's a breakdown of the game's standout features and what sets it apart from its predecessors.

1. Open-World Exploration Across the Hawaiian Archipelago

For the first time in the series, players can explore a vast, open-world environment that extends beyond urban streets to the **tropical islands and ocean waters of Hawaii**. The game features:

- **Multiple Islands to Discover:** From bustling **Honolulu** to the lawless pirate haven of **Madlantis**, and the mysterious **Nele Island**, each location offers unique environments, cultures, and hidden secrets.
- **Dynamic Environments:** Experience **lush jungles, bustling coastal cities, treacherous caves, and even underwater ruins**. Dynamic weather and a day-night cycle affect gameplay, with certain missions or events triggered by specific conditions.
- **Seamless Land-to-Sea Transition:** No loading screens between sailing and docking—**just hop off your ship and dive straight into the action.**

2. Dual Combat Styles: Mad Dog & Sea Dog

Majima's combat prowess has been reimagined with two distinct fighting styles, allowing players to adapt to different situations:

- **Mad Dog Style:** A nod to Majima's classic fighting style—fast, erratic, and brutal. This style focuses on **quick strikes, agile dodging, and acrobatic combos**, perfect for one-on-one battles and chaotic brawls.
- **Sea Dog Style:** A new pirate-themed combat mode where Majima wields **dual cutlasses, pistols, and improvised**

pirate weaponry. This style emphasizes **wide-range attacks, gunplay, and powerful finishing moves**, ideal for crowd control and naval skirmishes.

- **Aerial Combat Mechanics:** For the first time, players can perform **jump attacks, mid-air combos, and environmental takedowns**, adding a new layer of depth to the traditional beat 'em up formula.

3. Naval Exploration & Real-Time Ship Battles

One of the game's most exciting additions is the ability to **sail the open seas aboard Majima's ship, the *Goromaru***. This feature introduces:

- **Real-Time Naval Combat:** Engage in epic ship battles where you can **fire cannons, board enemy vessels, and lead deck brawls**. Tactics matter—**positioning, crew management, and ship upgrades** are key to victory.
- **Ship Customization:** Upgrade the *Goromaru* with **new weapons, reinforced hulls, faster sails, and decorative flair** to suit your pirate aesthetic.
- **Crew Recruitment:** Assemble a diverse crew of outlaws, each with unique abilities that enhance ship performance or aid in combat.

4. A Rich, Story-Driven Experience with Multiple Paths

True to the *Like a Dragon* legacy, the game offers an emotionally charged narrative filled with **complex characters, shocking plot twists, and moral choices** that affect the story's outcome:

- **Non-Linear Story Progression:** Players can choose which missions to tackle first, leading to **branching storylines** and multiple possible endings.
- **Dynamic Dialogue Choices:** Conversations are more interactive, allowing Majima's responses to shape relationships with allies, enemies, and crew members.
- **Themed Side Quests:** In addition to the main story, quirky side missions range from **hunting mythical sea creatures to solving crimes in pirate-run towns**—all packed with the series' trademark humor and heart.

5. Expanded Mini-Games and Side Activities

No *Like a Dragon* game would be complete without over-the-top mini-games, and this entry takes things to the next level with both returning favorites and new pirate-themed activities:

- **Karaoke (Pirate Edition):** Sing sea shanties and classic Yakuza tracks—with Majima's unique flair, of course.
- **Dragon Kart Returns:** Race pirate-themed go-karts through tropical tracks filled with hazards, power-ups, and rival racers.
- **Crazy Delivery:** A chaotic delivery mini-game where Majima races to deliver goods across the islands, dodging obstacles and pirates.
- **Treasure Hunts & Diving:** Use maps and clues to uncover hidden treasures, or **dive underwater** to explore sunken ruins and shipwrecks.

6. RPG Elements and Crew Management

Expanding on the RPG mechanics introduced in *Yakuza: Like a Dragon*, this game allows players to manage not just Majima's growth, but his entire crew:

- **Crew Management System:** Recruit pirates, assign them roles (combat specialist, navigator, mechanic), and **manage their morale and loyalty.**
- **Character Progression:** Upgrade Majima's skills through **combat experience, leadership decisions, and even pirate-themed training sessions.**
- **Resource Gathering & Crafting:** Collect resources from islands to **craft weapons, upgrade gear, and improve your ship.**

7. Hidden Secrets, Easter Eggs, and Post-Game Content

Fans of the series know to expect plenty of hidden gems, and *Pirate Yakuza in Hawaii* delivers:

- **Secret Boss Battles:** Face off against **mythical sea creatures, legendary pirates, and surprise characters from past Yakuza games.**
- **Easter Eggs:** Packed with **references to previous *Like a Dragon* titles**, Sega classics, and Majima's own chaotic history.
- **New Game+ Mode:** Replay the story with **all upgrades, unlockables, and hidden challenges** to discover post-game content.

1.4 Understanding the Yakuza Legacy in a Pirate Setting

The Evolution of the Yakuza Series

The *Like a Dragon* (formerly *Yakuza*) series has always been known for its **gritty crime dramas, deep character development, and explosive street-fighting mechanics** set against the backdrop of Japan's urban underworld. From Kamurocho's neon lights to Ijincho's bustling alleys, the series has masterfully combined **serious, emotionally driven narratives** with **over-the-top side activities** and unforgettable characters.

However, *Like a Dragon: Pirate Yakuza in Hawaii* represents a bold leap—a transition from city streets to the **open seas and tropical islands**. Despite this drastic change in setting, the game remains firmly rooted in the **core themes and values that define the franchise**.

Core Yakuza Themes in a Pirate World

While the setting has shifted from modern Japan to the pirate-infested waters of Hawaii, many of the franchise's hallmark themes remain intact:

1. **Honor Among Thieves:**
   Just like the traditional Yakuza code, the pirate factions in the game operate under their own **codes of honor and loyalty**. Majima, though no longer tied to the Tojo Clan, still embodies these principles, navigating **alliances and betrayals** in a world where trust is a rare currency.
2. **Found Family & Brotherhood:**
   The *Yakuza* series has always explored the concept of

family beyond blood ties. In this game, Majima forms his own pirate crew, forging bonds with outcasts, rogues, and unlikely allies, much like Kiryu's relationships with his comrades in previous titles.

3. **The Struggle for Identity:**
   Majima's journey mirrors the internal conflicts faced by past protagonists. **Stranded with no memory of his past**, he grapples with questions of identity, purpose, and destiny—a recurring theme throughout the series.

4. **Power, Corruption, and Redemption:**
   Whether it's the corrupt Yakuza clans of Kamurocho or the ruthless pirate lords of Hawaii, the game delves into the **dynamics of power and the consequences of ambition**, forcing Majima to confront not just external enemies, but his own moral compass.

Majima: A Yakuza Icon in Uncharted Waters

Goro Majima's presence is the perfect bridge between the old and new. As the "Mad Dog of Shimano," he's always thrived in chaos, making him the ideal character to thrive in this unpredictable pirate setting.

- **Unpredictability Fits the Pirate Life:** Majima's chaotic energy, wild fighting style, and unorthodox methods make him feel **right at home in a lawless, pirate-dominated world.**
- **From Tojo Clan Lieutenant to Pirate Captain:** While he's no longer bound by Yakuza politics, his **leadership skills, street smarts, and fierce loyalty** seamlessly transition to his role as a pirate captain.
- **A Personal Quest:** Unlike Kiryu's often noble, stoic journeys, Majima's adventure is **raw, personal, and driven**

by both **survival and self-discovery**, making his character arc feel fresh yet familiar.

Blending Modern Yakuza Culture with Historical Pirate Lore

The game cleverly fuses the **modern crime elements of the Yakuza world with the romanticized chaos of pirate lore**:

- **Rival Factions = Pirate Crews:** Instead of Yakuza families like the Omi Alliance or Tojo Clan, Majima faces off against **rival pirate captains and seafaring crime syndicates**, each with distinct codes, rivalries, and territories.
- **Territory Control Reimagined:** Previously tied to city turf wars, the concept is now applied to **island strongholds and naval dominance**, where players can **capture ports, raid enemy ships, and expand their influence across the Hawaiian archipelago.**
- **Business Management → Crew Management:** The beloved business management mechanics from past games evolve into **pirate crew recruitment and ship management**, where loyalty, morale, and strategic planning play key roles.

The Yakuza Humor & Quirkiness Still Intact

Despite the shift in tone and setting, the franchise's signature **quirky side content, bizarre mini-games, and laugh-out-loud moments** remain:

- **Outrageous Side Quests:** From **helping ghost pirates find peace** to **participating in absurd pirate talent shows**, the side quests maintain the series' beloved eccentricity.

- **Mini-Games with a Pirate Twist:** Karaoke with sea shanties? Check. **Pirate-themed Dragon Kart racing** through volcanic islands? Absolutely. Even **sword duels with overly dramatic villains** are part of the fun.
- **Easter Eggs for Longtime Fans:** Expect references to **Kamurocho, the Tojo Clan, and even past characters** subtly woven into dialogue, items, and hidden quests.

Chapter 2: Characters and Factions

2.1 Goro Majima: The Mad Dog of the High Seas

Goro Majima, the unpredictable and charismatic "Mad Dog of Shimano," takes center stage in *Like a Dragon: Pirate Yakuza in Hawaii*. Known for his wild antics, chaotic fighting style, and fierce loyalty, Majima has always been a standout character in the *Like a Dragon* series. This time, he trades the back alleys of Kamurocho for the vast, lawless waters of the Pacific, embarking on a new journey that blends his notorious madness with the ruthless life of a pirate captain.

Majima's New Role: From Yakuza Lieutenant to Pirate Captain

In previous games, Majima thrived as a lieutenant of the Tojo Clan, known for his violent tendencies and unpredictable behavior. In *Pirate Yakuza in Hawaii*, however, Majima finds himself in uncharted territory—literally and figuratively. After waking up shipwrecked on an unknown island with no memory of how he got there, Majima must rely on his instincts, survival skills, and sheer willpower to rise through the ranks of Hawaii's pirate underworld.

He quickly earns a reputation as a **fearsome pirate captain**, commanding his own ship, the **Goromaru**, and assembling a diverse crew of outlaws and misfits. Despite being far from his Yakuza roots,

Majima's natural leadership, cunning mind, and chaotic energy make him a force to be reckoned with both on land and at sea.

Personality: Chaos, Loyalty, and Hidden Depths

Majima is defined by his **dual nature**—on the surface, he's a wild, unhinged, and often hilarious figure, but beneath the madness lies a deeply loyal, strategic, and emotionally complex individual. In *Pirate Yakuza in Hawaii*, this complexity is explored even further:

- **Unpredictable but Strategic:** While Majima thrives in chaos, he's far from reckless. His ability to adapt to any situation, whether it's a street brawl or a naval skirmish, makes him a master tactician in disguise.
- **Fierce Loyalty:** Loyalty has always been at Majima's core. Even in this new pirate world, he forms **deep bonds with his crew**, treating them like family. His protective nature often leads to intense emotional moments amidst the game's chaos.
- **Search for Identity:** Stripped of his past and thrust into an unfamiliar world, Majima's journey isn't just about survival or treasure—it's about **rediscovering who he truly is** when everything he once knew is gone.

Combat Style: Mad Dog Meets Sea Dog

Majima's combat style is as wild and versatile as ever, blending his iconic techniques with new pirate-themed abilities:

- **Mad Dog Style:** A fast, aggressive fighting style characterized by **acrobatic moves, dual-wielded weapons, and erratic attack patterns**. This style focuses on overwhelming enemies with speed and unpredictability.

- **Sea Dog Style:** A new pirate-inspired combat mode where Majima uses **cutlasses, flintlock pistols, and improvised seafaring weapons**. This style excels in crowd control and adds a theatrical flair to his already dynamic battles.
- **Environmental Combat:** Majima can now **use the environment to his advantage**, swinging from ship riggings, kicking barrels at enemies, or even launching surprise attacks from underwater.

Character Development: A Pirate's Journey of Self-Discovery

While Majima has always been a fan favorite for his wild antics, *Pirate Yakuza in Hawaii* delves deeper into his **personal growth and emotional struggles**:

- **Lost Memories:** The game's central mystery revolves around Majima's missing memories. As he uncovers the truth, players witness a side of him rarely seen— **vulnerable, reflective, and haunted by the past**.
- **Leadership Growth:** Majima's role as a pirate captain forces him to take on new responsibilities, challenging him to **balance his chaotic nature with the need to inspire and protect his crew**.
- **Moral Choices:** Throughout the story, players will make decisions that shape Majima's relationships and the course of his journey, highlighting the **gray areas between honor and survival** in the pirate world.

2.2 Supporting Characters and Crew Members

In *Like a Dragon: Pirate Yakuza in Hawaii*, Goro Majima isn't sailing the high seas alone. As he navigates the treacherous waters of the Hawaiian archipelago, he assembles a **colorful and diverse crew**, each with their own unique backstories, skills, and motivations. These supporting characters are more than just sidekicks—they're integral to Majima's journey, contributing to both the gameplay mechanics and the emotional depth of the story.

The Role of the Crew in Majima's Journey

Majima's crew isn't just a ragtag band of outlaws; they represent **family, loyalty, and survival** in a world where betrayal is always lurking. Each crew member adds a new dynamic to the narrative, challenging Majima's leadership while providing critical support during both land-based combat and naval battles.

Crew members also play a key role in the **Crew Management System**, where their unique abilities influence ship performance, combat efficiency, and even the outcome of certain story events. Building strong relationships with them can unlock **special missions, hidden abilities, and powerful loyalty bonuses**.

Key Supporting Characters and Crew Members

1. Hana "Crimson Blade" Tanaka – First Mate

- **Background:** A former Yakuza enforcer from Osaka, Hana left the criminal underworld after being betrayed by her own clan. Sharp-tongued and fiercely independent, she crosses paths with Majima after a heated bar brawl in a pirate den. Impressed by her combat skills and tactical mind, Majima recruits her as his first mate.

- **Personality: Cynical, strategic, and secretly compassionate.** She keeps Majima grounded, often acting as the voice of reason amidst his chaos. Despite her tough exterior, she deeply values loyalty and gradually becomes Majima's closest confidante.
- **Combat Role:** A **blade master** specializing in dual katanas. Her attacks are fast and precise, making her invaluable during close-quarters combat.
- **Unique Ability: "Crimson Frenzy"** – Unleashes a flurry of slashes, dealing massive damage to multiple enemies in quick succession.

2. Kimo "Sharkbait" Kalani – Navigator

- **Background:** Born and raised in a small Hawaiian fishing village, Kimo was orphaned after a pirate raid destroyed his home. He grew up learning to navigate the treacherous Pacific waters, eventually becoming one of the most skilled sailors in the archipelago. Majima saves him from a rival pirate crew, earning his lifelong loyalty.
- **Personality: Easygoing, superstitious, and loyal.** Kimo believes in island folklore and often tells exaggerated tales of sea monsters and ancient curses. His humor and laid-back attitude provide comic relief during tense moments.
- **Combat Role:** A **ranged specialist** using harpoons and throwable explosives. While not as strong in melee combat, he's perfect for providing support from a distance.
- **Unique Ability: "Tidal Barrage"** – Launches a volley of explosive harpoons, dealing area-of-effect damage to enemies on both land and sea.

3. Dr. Emiliano "Doc" Vargas – Ship's Surgeon

- **Background:** A disgraced Spanish naval doctor turned rogue pirate, Doc Vargas is a genius with a dark past. He fled the mainland after being accused of illegal experiments, finding refuge among pirates where his medical skills are both feared and respected. Majima discovers him running an underground clinic in Honolulu.
- **Personality: Mysterious, morbidly humorous, and morally ambiguous.** Vargas is fascinated by human anatomy and isn't shy about discussing gruesome medical details, much to the discomfort of the crew. Despite his creepy demeanor, he's surprisingly loyal and protective.
- **Combat Role:** A **support class** specializing in healing, buffs, and poisons. He can both heal allies and debilitate enemies with toxic concoctions.
- **Unique Ability: "Reaper's Remedy"** – Simultaneously heals allies and poisons nearby enemies, creating a deadly dual effect during battle.

4. Tane "Iron Fist" Mahoe – Quartermaster

- **Background:** A former heavyweight boxing champion from Honolulu, Tane was exiled from the fighting circuit after a scandal involving rigged matches. Struggling to survive, he turned to piracy, using his brute strength to intimidate rivals. Majima challenges and defeats him in an underground fight, earning his respect and allegiance.
- **Personality: Stoic, disciplined, and fiercely honorable.** Tane is a man of few words, preferring to let his fists do the talking. He serves as the crew's moral compass, often challenging Majima's decisions when they cross ethical lines.

- **Combat Role:** A **heavy-hitter** specializing in unarmed combat. His raw power allows him to **stagger large enemies** and break through shields with ease.
- **Unique Ability: "Titan's Wrath"** – A devastating ground-pound attack that creates shockwaves, knocking down multiple enemies in the area.

Dynamic Crew Relationships

The relationships Majima builds with his crew are dynamic and evolve based on **player choices, story progression, and loyalty missions.** Crew members will:

- **React to Majima's Decisions:** Certain choices can either strengthen or strain relationships, leading to unique dialogue, confrontations, or even betrayal in extreme cases.
- **Unlock Loyalty Missions:** Completing personal side quests for each crew member reveals their backstories, deepens their bond with Majima, and unlocks powerful combat abilities.
- **Impact Ship Performance:** A well-managed crew with high morale will improve the *Goromaru's* speed, combat efficiency, and defense during naval battles.

Crew Management System

Outside of combat, players can engage with the **Crew Management System**, where Majima can:

- **Assign Roles:** Designate crew members as **combat specialists, navigators, gunners, or medics**, affecting how the ship performs in different scenarios.

- **Upgrade Skills:** Spend experience points to unlock new abilities for each crew member, enhancing their effectiveness in battle.
- **Boost Morale:** Participate in activities like **crew dinners, drinking games, and training sessions** to boost team morale, which in turn improves performance during missions.

Memorable Side Characters

Beyond the main crew, Majima encounters a host of memorable NPCs, including:

- **Rival Pirate Captains** with distinct personalities, fighting styles, and territories to defend.
- **Shady Merchants** who offer rare items and questionable deals.
- **Mysterious Strangers** who may hold clues about Majima's lost memories or hidden treasures.

2.3 Pirate Factions and Rival Gangs

In *Like a Dragon: Pirate Yakuza in Hawaii*, the seas are not just vast stretches of water—they're battlegrounds ruled by **powerful pirate factions and ruthless rival gangs**. Each faction controls different territories across the Hawaiian archipelago, from bustling island ports to hidden coves and treacherous waters. These groups aren't just enemies; they represent the complex political landscape that Majima must navigate to survive, thrive, and ultimately dominate as a pirate captain.

Understanding the **hierarchy, motives, and personalities** within these factions is key to both the game's story and its strategic gameplay. Whether it's through brutal naval warfare, tense negotiations, or personal vendettas, Majima's encounters with these factions will shape the course of his pirate odyssey.

The Power Dynamics of Hawaii's Pirate Underworld

The Hawaiian archipelago is divided among **four dominant pirate factions**, each with its own culture, leadership style, and combat strategies. While they all share a thirst for power and treasure, their approaches vary—from honor-bound codes to outright anarchy.

Majima's relationship with these factions isn't static. Depending on the player's choices, he can:

- **Forge alliances** for mutual benefit.
- **Instigate turf wars** to expand his influence.
- **Betray former allies** for personal gain.
- **Unite factions** under his banner—or destroy them completely.

Major Pirate Factions

1. The Crimson Lotus Fleet

- **Territory:** Eastern Hawaiian waters, controlling major trade routes and coastal settlements.
- **Leader: Captain Akane "Scarlet Viper" Fujiwara** – A former samurai turned pirate queen, known for her deadly precision and strict code of honor. She wields a **katana dipped in crimson lacquer**, rumored to have been stained with the blood of her enemies.
- **Philosophy: "Honor Above All."** The Crimson Lotus operates like a disciplined naval force, blending samurai

traditions with pirate tactics. They believe in structured hierarchies and view themselves as "noble pirates."

- **Strengths:** Highly organized, with elite swordsmen and disciplined naval strategies. Their ships are fast, agile, and equipped with advanced weaponry.
- **Relationship with Majima:** Initially hostile, viewing Majima as a chaotic threat to their order. However, **earning Akane's respect through honorable combat** can open the door to an uneasy alliance.

2. The Iron Fang Brotherhood

- **Territory:** The volcanic islands of the western archipelago, fortified with hidden strongholds and smuggling routes.
- **Leader: Bartholomew "Iron Jaw" Kane** – A towering brute with a mechanical jaw, Kane is a former slave-turned-pirate warlord. His obsession with power is matched only by his brutality.
- **Philosophy: "Strength Rules All."** The Iron Fang Brotherhood thrives on fear, violence, and intimidation. They believe the strong should dominate the weak, and they enforce this belief through relentless raids and extortion.
- **Strengths:** Specializes in **brute force**, with heavily armored ships and berserker warriors who rely on sheer physical dominance.
- **Relationship with Majima:** A natural rivalry forms due to their conflicting leadership styles. However, **Majima can challenge Kane's authority** by defeating his lieutenants, potentially taking control of parts of the Brotherhood for himself.

3. The Black Tide Syndicate

- **Territory:** The bustling port city of Honolulu and its surrounding waters, controlling black markets, espionage networks, and corrupt officials.
- **Leader: Isabella "The Siren" Moreau** – A seductive and manipulative crime lord who hides her cruelty behind charm and wit. She's a master of deception, playing allies and enemies alike like pieces on a chessboard.
- **Philosophy: "Profit Over Loyalty."** The Black Tide operates more like a criminal syndicate than a traditional pirate crew, focusing on smuggling, information brokering, and political manipulation.
- **Strengths:** Masters of **espionage and sabotage**, with spies hidden in every major port. Their ships are fast, perfect for smuggling and hit-and-run tactics.
- **Relationship with Majima:** Isabella sees Majima as both a potential pawn and a dangerous wild card. Players can **engage in risky alliances, double-crosses, and espionage missions**, but betrayal is always a looming threat.

4. The Ghost Reef Corsairs

- **Territory:** The uncharted waters around the treacherous Ghost Reef, rumored to be cursed. They control hidden coves and secret islands that don't appear on any map.
- **Leader: Captain "Deadeye" Rua Koa** – A mysterious, masked pirate whose past is shrouded in legend. Some say he's immortal, others claim he's a ghost. His crew believes he's a living embodiment of the sea's wrath.
- **Philosophy: "Chaos Is Freedom."** The Ghost Reef Corsairs embrace anarchy, living by no code except the pursuit of freedom. They are unpredictable, attacking both allies and enemies without warning.

- **Strengths: Guerrilla warfare tactics**, using the environment to their advantage. Their ships are modified for stealth, perfect for ambushes and hit-and-run assaults.
- **Relationship with Majima:** A wild card faction— sometimes allies, sometimes enemies. **Majima's own chaotic nature resonates with Rua Koa**, creating a rivalry filled with mutual respect and inevitable betrayal.

Rival Gangs and Minor Factions

Beyond the major pirate factions, Hawaii is home to **smaller gangs, mercenary groups, and local militias**. While not as powerful, these groups can pose significant threats—or become valuable allies.

- **The Bone Rats:** A savage gang of raiders known for ambushing isolated ships. They worship a twisted version of ancient Hawaiian sea gods, believing piracy is a sacred act.
- **The Silver Serpents:** A mercenary crew that works for the highest bidder, often switching allegiances mid-battle if it benefits them.
- **The Crimson Traders:** A shadowy organization controlling illegal trade routes. They prefer manipulation and sabotage over direct conflict.
- **Local Island Militias:** Not all resistance comes from pirates. Some island communities have formed militias to protect themselves from constant raids. Players can **choose to help or exploit these groups** for personal gain.

Faction Reputation System

Your actions directly impact how factions perceive Majima. This dynamic system influences:

- **Alliances and Rivalries:** Gain favor with one faction, and you might become an enemy to another.
- **Turf Control:** Successfully defeating rival factions allows Majima to **claim territory**, earning resources, crew members, and strategic advantages.
- **Unique Missions:** High reputation unlocks **faction-specific side quests**, special rewards, and even the chance to recruit powerful faction leaders.
- **Betrayal Consequences:** Double-crossing a faction can lead to **ambushes, bounty hunters, and large-scale faction wars**.

Naval Warfare and Faction Conflicts

The faction system isn't just for storytelling—it's deeply woven into the gameplay:

- **Turf Wars:** Engage in **large-scale naval battles** where players command their fleet against enemy factions, capturing strongholds and ports.
- **Espionage Missions:** Infiltrate enemy camps, **assassinate key leaders**, or steal valuable resources.
- **Diplomatic Encounters:** Negotiate fragile truces or **intimidate rival captains** through dialogue choices, with outcomes shaped by Majima's reputation.

Legendary Pirate Captains (Boss Battles)

Each faction is led by a **legendary pirate captain**, serving as major bosses in the game. These encounters aren't just about brute force—they require players to understand the captain's tactics, faction strengths, and weaknesses:

- **Captain Akane's Duel of Honor:** A one-on-one katana duel atop a burning ship.
- **Bartholomew Kane's Arena Brawl:** A brutal cage match surrounded by his bloodthirsty crew.
- **Isabella Moreau's Deception:** A battle laced with psychological mind games and ambush traps.
- **Deadeye Rua Koa's Ghost Ship Showdown:** A supernatural fight aboard a cursed ship lost in a deadly fog.

2.4 Allies, Enemies, and NPC Interactions

In *Like a Dragon: Pirate Yakuza in Hawaii*, the world feels alive not just because of its vibrant settings and thrilling battles, but due to the **dynamic relationships Majima forms with allies, enemies, and a diverse range of NPCs**. These interactions are more than just background filler—they actively shape the narrative, unlock side quests, and impact gameplay mechanics. Whether Majima is forging alliances, engaging in brutal rivalries, or simply having bizarre encounters with eccentric locals, every interaction adds depth to his pirate odyssey.

The Role of NPCs in Majima's Journey

NPCs (Non-Playable Characters) are critical to both the story and gameplay. They serve various roles:

- **Allies** who fight alongside Majima, offering unique skills and emotional depth.
- **Enemies** who create tension, conflict, and memorable boss battles.
- **Neutral NPCs** who offer side quests, sell rare items, or provide world-building lore.

- **Dynamic Characters** whose relationships with Majima evolve based on player choices, actions, and reputation within different factions.

Allies: Friends in a Lawless World

While Majima thrives on chaos, even the "Mad Dog" needs a crew he can rely on. Beyond his core team, *Like a Dragon: Pirate Yakuza in Hawaii* introduces a variety of **allies who join Majima's cause temporarily or become recurring companions** throughout the game.

Key Allies Outside the Main Crew

1. **Detective Keoni Matsuoka**
   - **Role:** A morally conflicted detective with the Honolulu Harbor Authority, Keoni starts as an adversary investigating Majima's pirate activities but eventually becomes an unlikely ally.
   - **Personality: Stoic, principled, and haunted by personal loss.** His sense of justice often clashes with Majima's chaotic methods, creating a tense but compelling partnership.
   - **Gameplay Impact:** Assists during **investigation missions**, unlocking hidden information, infiltration tactics, and crime-solving mini-games.
2. **Lani "Storm Whisper" Keawe**
   - **Role:** A rebellious freedom fighter leading a small militia against oppressive pirate factions and corrupt colonial forces.
   - **Personality: Passionate, fearless, and driven by vengeance.** Lani challenges Majima's morals, often pushing him to consider the consequences of his actions beyond personal gain.

- Gameplay Impact: Unlocks **guerrilla warfare missions**, sabotage operations, and access to unique weapons crafted from island resources.

3. **Hiroshi "Slim" Nakamura**
   - **Role:** A former Tojo Clan informant who fled to Hawaii after betraying the wrong people. Slim offers Majima crucial information about **Yakuza connections** hidden within the pirate networks.
   - **Personality: Slick, cowardly, but surprisingly resourceful.** He's always looking out for himself but proves useful when the stakes are high.
   - **Gameplay Impact:** Provides access to **black market deals**, espionage missions, and intelligence on rival factions.

4. **Captain Pua "Steel Wave" Mahina**
   - **Role:** A respected leader of an indigenous seafaring tribe, Pua's mastery of the ocean rivals even the fiercest pirates.
   - **Personality: Wise, reserved, and spiritually connected to the sea.** Pua serves as both an ally and mentor, helping Majima understand the cultural significance of Hawaii's islands.
   - **Gameplay Impact:** Enhances **naval combat mechanics**, offering upgrades for Majima's ship and teaching advanced sailing techniques.

Enemies: Rivals, Betrayers, and Legends

No pirate story is complete without formidable foes, and Majima's journey is filled with enemies who test his strength, wit, and resilience. These adversaries range from **rival pirate captains to personal vendettas rooted in Majima's past.**

Notable Antagonists

1. **Victor "The Vulture" DeMarco**
   - **Role:** A sadistic pirate slaver who profits from human trafficking across the Pacific. Victor thrives on psychological manipulation, often taunting Majima with mind games.
   - **Personality: Cruel, intelligent, and ruthlessly efficient.** He enjoys breaking people both physically and mentally.
   - **Boss Fight:** A brutal battle aboard a slave galley, filled with environmental hazards like collapsing decks and explosive barrels.

2. **Lieutenant Kaito "The Serpent" Sugimura**
   - **Role:** A high-ranking Yakuza member with ties to Majima's lost memories. Kaito operates in the shadows, orchestrating events from behind the scenes.
   - **Personality: Calculating, cold, and manipulative.** Unlike Majima's chaotic energy, Kaito is methodical and patient, making him a terrifying contrast.
   - **Boss Fight:** A tactical duel in an underground Yakuza hideout, where Kaito uses **traps, ambushes, and psychological warfare** against Majima.

3. **Captain Rua "Deadeye" Koa (Rival Pirate Lord)**
   - **Role:** Leader of the Ghost Reef Corsairs, Rua is both a rival and a twisted reflection of Majima's own chaotic nature. Their relationship oscillates between mutual respect and deadly rivalry.
   - **Personality: Mysterious, philosophical, and dangerously unpredictable.** Rua believes in the freedom chaos brings, making him a compelling foil to Majima.

- **Boss Fight:** A legendary naval battle during a raging storm, with **boarding sequences** that shift from ship-to-ship cannon fire to close-quarters sword fights.

4. **The "Crimson Widow" Akane Fujiwara (Faction Leader)**
    - **Role:** Head of the Crimson Lotus Fleet, Akane's rigid code of honor puts her at odds with Majima's lawless ways.
    - **Personality: Disciplined, fierce, and unwavering.** Akane is one of the few who can match Majima's skill in a one-on-one fight.
    - **Boss Fight:** A katana duel at sunset on a burning dock, with environmental hazards and cinematic finishers.

NPC Interaction System

The game features a **robust NPC interaction system** that affects both narrative and gameplay. These interactions range from light-hearted side quests to pivotal story decisions with lasting consequences.

Key Features of the NPC Interaction System:

1. **Dynamic Dialogue Choices**
    - Conversations often present players with multiple responses, ranging from **intimidation, persuasion, or humor**.
    - Choices impact relationships, unlock hidden quests, or trigger unique reactions from NPCs.
    - Some decisions can even lead to **unexpected betrayals or alliances** later in the game.

2. **Reputation and Influence**
   - ○ Majima's reputation affects how NPCs interact with him.
   - ○ A **fearsome reputation** might cause enemies to surrender without a fight, while a **charismatic approach** opens doors to diplomatic solutions.
   - ○ Factions and neutral NPCs track Majima's reputation, influencing **trade deals, recruitment opportunities, and access to restricted areas.**
3. **Side Quests and Substories**
   - ○ Classic to the *Like a Dragon* series, quirky and emotional **substories** return with a pirate twist.
   - ○ Players might help a **lovesick sailor woo a mermaid (or at least someone dressed like one)**, uncover **ancient island curses**, or solve **bizarre local mysteries.**
   - ○ Completing side quests often rewards players with **rare items, skill upgrades, or new crew members**.
4. **Bonds and Loyalty Mechanics**
   - ○ Building strong bonds with allies unlocks **"Loyalty Skills,"** powerful abilities that trigger during combat when fighting alongside specific characters.
   - ○ Spending time with NPCs through activities like **drinking, sparring, or participating in crew events** deepens these relationships.
   - ○ Some characters may even have **romantic subplots**, adding emotional layers to the story.

Special NPC Encounters

- **Mysterious Hermits:** Found on remote islands, offering cryptic wisdom or rare treasures in exchange for completing strange challenges.

- **Bounty Hunters:** NPCs hired by rival factions to track and eliminate Majima. These encounters trigger **dynamic ambush events** both on land and at sea.
- **Legendary Traders:** Eccentric merchants who sell **one-of-a-kind weapons, ancient artifacts, and rare ship upgrades**, often hidden in hard-to-reach locations.

Humor and Eccentric Characters

True to the *Like a Dragon* series, the game doesn't shy away from bizarre, hilarious NPC interactions. Expect:

- A **pirate karaoke bar** where Majima sings sea shanties with dramatic flair.
- A **talking parrot NPC** that dispenses life advice and occasionally insults Majima.
- A quest involving a **"haunted" coconut** believed to be cursed (spoiler: it's just a regular coconut).

Chapter 3: Gameplay Mechanics

3.1 Core Combat System Explained

In *Like a Dragon: Pirate Yakuza in Hawaii*, the combat system evolves beyond traditional street brawls, blending **classic Yakuza-style beat-'em-up mechanics** with dynamic, pirate-themed action. Players will engage in intense **hand-to-hand combat, sword fights, naval skirmishes, and even chaotic brawls aboard sinking ships**. The game seamlessly merges fast-paced combos with environmental interactions, making every fight feel fresh, brutal, and cinematic.

Key Elements of the Core Combat System

1. Real-Time Action Combat

The game retains the real-time combat fans love, with smooth transitions between exploration and fighting.

- **Fluid Combos:** Mix light and heavy attacks to create devastating combos.
- **Counter Attacks:** Perfectly timed blocks or dodges trigger brutal counterattacks.
- **Heat Actions:** Over-the-top, cinematic finishers triggered when Majima's **Heat Gauge** is full. Expect wild pirate-themed finishers like **impaling enemies with harpoons** or smashing heads with **rum barrels**.

2. Environmental Combat

Majima's chaotic energy shines through environmental interactions.

- **Use Objects as Weapons:** Bar stools, anchors, oars, coconuts—you name it, Majima can weaponize it.
- **Dynamic Arenas:** Fights take place on unstable ships, docks with collapsing planks, and taverns where tables can be smashed into splinters.
- **Naval Combat Integration:** Transition seamlessly from deck brawls to cannon control during ship battles.

3. Combo Chain System

A new **Combo Chain System** rewards aggressive playstyles:

- **Chain Bonuses:** String together melee, ranged, and environmental attacks without taking damage to boost Majima's attack power.
- **Combo Finishers:** Unlock unique moves when reaching high combo counts, such as **spinning sword slashes** or **dual-pistol acrobatics**.

4. Weapon Versatility

Majima isn't limited to fists. The game features a wide array of pirate-era weapons:

- **Melee Weapons:** Cutlasses, katanas, boarding axes, and even broken bottles.
- **Ranged Weapons:** Flintlock pistols, throwing knives, muskets, and improvised firearms like **cannon pistols**.
- **Dual-Wielding:** Some weapons can be dual-wielded, allowing for flashy, high-speed attacks.

5. Adrenaline Surge Mode

Replacing the traditional "Rage Mode," Majima can enter **Adrenaline Surge** when his meter fills:

- **Slowed Time:** Time briefly slows, letting Majima chain rapid attacks.
- **Enhanced Damage:** Attacks deal increased damage, with unique animations.
- **Unlimited Heat Actions:** While active, Majima can spam Heat Actions without restrictions.

3.2 Mad Dog vs. Sea Dog Fighting Styles

Majima's signature unpredictability extends to his dual fighting styles: **Mad Dog** and **Sea Dog**. Players can switch between these styles mid-combat, each offering distinct strengths, weaknesses, and mechanics.

Mad Dog Fighting Style (Returning from Yakuza Series)

Majima's iconic, chaotic brawler style returns with enhancements tailored for pirate combat.

- **Speed & Ferocity:** Fast, erratic movements with relentless aggression.
- **Weapon Integration:** Focus on **bladed weapons** like katanas and knives, with spinning attacks and quick slashes.
- **Acrobatic Maneuvers:** Dodge flips, wall-kicks, and unpredictable lunges to keep enemies off-balance.
- **Signature Move: "Mad Dog Frenzy"**—a berserk mode where Majima unleashes a flurry of slashes while laughing maniacally.

Best Used Against:

- Fast, agile enemies.
- In tight spaces like ship interiors or crowded bars.

Sea Dog Fighting Style (New for Pirate Setting)

Inspired by traditional pirate brawling, Sea Dog focuses on **brute strength, naval weapons, and environmental interactions**.

- **Heavy Strikes:** Slower, but devastating attacks using **axes, harpoons, and blunt weapons**.
- **Grappling Techniques:** Command grabs, throws, and wrestling moves—perfect for **tossing enemies overboard**.
- **Cannon Fury:** Special moves where Majima literally **fires handheld cannons** at close range.
- **Signature Move: "Anchor Smash"**—Majima swings an anchor like a giant flail, dealing massive area damage.

Best Used Against:

- Armored foes and large enemy groups.
- During shipboard battles where environmental hazards can be exploited.

Switching Styles Mid-Combat

- **Seamless Transitions:** Swap between styles instantly to chain combos (e.g., starting with Mad Dog's fast strikes, then switching to Sea Dog for a powerful finisher).
- **Style-Specific Heat Actions:** Each style has unique Heat Moves, encouraging players to adapt based on the situation.

3.3 Jump Mechanics and Aerial Combos

For the first time in the *Like a Dragon* series, Majima's combat includes **jump mechanics and aerial combos**, adding a vertical dimension to fights. This isn't just for show—it's a game-changer, especially in pirate-themed environments with masts, rigging, and multi-level decks.

Jump Mechanics

- **Basic Jump:** A standard leap for dodging attacks or reaching elevated areas.
- **Wall Jumps:** In enclosed areas, Majima can **kick off walls** to gain height or perform surprise attacks.
- **Rope & Mast Navigation:** During ship battles, Majima can **swing from ropes** or **climb masts**, launching aerial attacks from above.

Aerial Combos

- **Launch Attacks:** Certain moves can **launch enemies into the air**, setting them up for aerial juggle combos.
- **Mid-Air Strikes:** Chain light and heavy attacks while airborne. Majima can **spin with dual cutlasses** or perform diving kicks.
- **Air Finishers:** Devastating moves that slam enemies back to the ground, causing shockwaves that damage surrounding foes.

Aerial Heat Actions

- **"Skull Diver Smash":** Majima leaps off a mast, driving his sword straight into an enemy's chest with a thunderous landing.
- **"Flying Mad Dog":** A ridiculous (and awesome) move where Majima somersaults mid-air, firing pistols in every direction before landing with a superhero pose.

Environmental Aerial Tactics

- **Ship Battles:** Jump between ships during naval combat or kick enemies off crow's nests.
- **Tavern Brawls:** Leap from balconies or chandeliers for surprise attacks.
- **Cliffside Duels:** Knock enemies off cliffs or ledges with dramatic slow-motion falls.

3.4 Health, Stamina, and Resource Management

Surviving the brutal world of pirate warfare isn't just about raw skill. Managing Majima's **health, stamina, and resources** is crucial, especially during extended battles and naval skirmishes.

Health System

- **Health Bar:** Standard health meter displayed on-screen. Damage reduces it, and depletion leads to defeat.
- **Injury Mechanic:** Taking heavy hits can cause **temporary injuries**, reducing maximum health until treated.
- **Regeneration:** Minor health regenerates slowly outside combat, but significant recovery requires items or abilities.

Stamina System

- **Stamina Bar:** Controls Majima's ability to sprint, dodge, and perform advanced maneuvers.
- **Exhaustion State:** Overusing stamina leads to temporary exhaustion, slowing Majima's movements.
- **Adrenaline Boost:** Landing consecutive hits without taking damage temporarily restores stamina faster.

Resource Management

1. Consumable Items

- **Health Potions:** Rum flasks, tropical fruits, and medicinal herbs restore health.
- **Stamina Tonics:** Energy drinks and pirate-themed concoctions boost stamina recovery.
- **Buff Items:** Temporary boosts to attack, defense, or speed. Example: **"Gunpowder Grog"** increases explosive damage.

2. Crafting Materials

- **Ship Upgrades:** Collect rare woods, metals, and sails to enhance your ship's stats.
- **Weapon Enhancements:** Gather materials to **sharpen swords, reinforce armor, or add elemental effects** to weapons.

3. Ammo Management (For Ranged Weapons)

- **Limited Ammo:** Firearms require careful ammo management. Players can scavenge or purchase bullets.
- **Special Ammo:** Unlock explosive rounds, poison-tipped darts, and incendiary cannonballs.

Status Effects

- **Bleeding:** Causes continuous health loss unless treated.
- **Burning:** Fire-based attacks set enemies (and sometimes Majima) ablaze, causing damage over time.
- **Drunken Rage:** Drinking too much alcohol in battle triggers unpredictable buffs—sometimes helpful, sometimes chaotic.

Healing Mechanics

- **Quick Heal:** Use items mid-combat through a quick-access menu.
- **Rest Points:** Safe zones like taverns or campfires allow full recovery and resource management.
- **Crew Support:** Certain allies can heal Majima during battle if their loyalty is high enough.

Chapter 4: Exploration and Open-World Navigation

4.1 Key Locations: Rich Island, Madlantis, Nele Island, and Honolulu

Like a Dragon: Pirate Yakuza in Hawaii features a sprawling open world set across the Pacific, blending **lush tropical islands, bustling pirate ports, ancient ruins, and urban environments**. Each key location offers unique stories, side quests, hidden secrets, and environmental challenges that push Majima's exploration skills to the limit.

Rich Island: The Pirate's Goldmine

- **Overview:** A tropical paradise corrupted by greed, Rich Island is the heart of pirate commerce in the region. Once a sacred land, it's now overrun with black markets, illegal trading posts, and rogue pirate factions battling for control.
- **Key Landmarks:**
    - **The Crimson Docks:** A chaotic harbor where ships unload contraband and rival pirates frequently clash.
    - **Gilded Market:** A bustling bazaar filled with exotic goods, rare weapons, and shady merchants.
    - **The Sunken Vault:** A hidden underground cavern rumored to house **ancient treasures** guarded by deadly traps.
- **Gameplay Highlights:**
    - **Intense gang battles** in the marketplace.

- Smuggling missions involving stealth and deception.
- Treasure hunts that require solving environmental puzzles.

Madlantis: The Lost City Beneath the Waves

- **Overview:** A mythic underwater city submerged after a volcanic eruption. Madlantis is a blend of **ancient ruins and advanced pirate technology**, with legends of cursed relics hidden within its depths.
- **Key Landmarks:**
  - **The Drowned Palace:** A maze-like structure filled with booby traps and spectral guardians.
  - **Coral Catacombs:** Labyrinthine tunnels populated by mutant sea creatures and scavenger pirates.
  - **The Leviathan's Graveyard:** A massive underwater battlefield surrounded by the bones of ancient sea beasts.
- **Gameplay Highlights:**
  - **Underwater exploration** using diving gear.
  - Solving **pressure-based puzzles** and avoiding underwater hazards.
  - Battling sea monsters in zero-gravity-like combat sequences.

Nele Island: The Savage Frontier

- **Overview:** Known as "The Island That Bites Back," Nele Island is a dense jungle filled with **untamed wildlife, hostile tribes, and dangerous terrain**. It's a lawless land where nature itself is Majima's enemy.
- **Key Landmarks:**

- - **Skull Rock Summit:** A towering cliff shaped like a skull, offering panoramic views and hidden sniping spots.
  - **The Hollow Grove:** A sacred forest where ancient spirits are said to roam—home to some of the game's most surreal side quests.
  - **Bloodwater Falls:** A waterfall concealing a secret cave system used by rebel pirates.
- **Gameplay Highlights:**
  - **Survival mechanics:** Crafting makeshift weapons, hunting for food, and avoiding environmental hazards like quicksand.
  - **Stealth-based missions** in dense foliage.
  - High-stakes chases with wild animals (yes, Majima can fistfight a bear if you're feeling brave).

Honolulu: The Pirate's Urban Playground

- **Overview:** A vibrant coastal city blending Hawaiian culture with colonial architecture. Unlike the lawless islands, Honolulu is heavily patrolled by naval authorities, creating tension for Majima as he navigates both the criminal underworld and high society.
- **Key Landmarks:**
  - **King's Row:** The luxurious district filled with colonial mansions, casinos, and political intrigue.
  - **The Slum Docks:** A gritty, dangerous area controlled by street gangs and rogue smugglers.
  - **The Royal Navy Fortress:** A heavily guarded military base that plays a key role in major story missions.
- **Gameplay Highlights:**
  - **Urban parkour** mechanics for rooftop chases.

- Engaging in **underground fight clubs** and illegal races.
- **Disguise system** to infiltrate enemy territories.

4.2 Fast Travel and Hidden Areas

Exploring the vast open world can be time-consuming, but the game offers **flexible fast travel options** while encouraging players to seek out hidden areas filled with rewards and surprises.

Fast Travel System

- **Port-to-Port Travel:** Unlockable **docks and harbors** serve as fast travel points. Majima can instantly sail between major islands once they've been discovered.
- **Secret Tunnels & Pirate Passages:** Hidden underground tunnels in cities like Honolulu allow for quick escapes or stealthy movement between districts.
- **Seafaring Taxi System:** A quirky fast-travel option where **eccentric sea captains** ferry Majima between islands, often with hilarious dialogue and side missions along the way.

Hidden Areas and Secret Locations

- **Treasure Coves:** Hidden caves filled with **rare loot**, guarded by traps or minibosses.
- **Lost Pirate Strongholds:** Abandoned fortresses that require solving environmental puzzles to access.
- **Mythical Shrines:** Mysterious altars connected to the game's supernatural elements. Offering items here can trigger **secret boss fights or hidden quests**.

- **Urban Secrets:** Rooftop hideouts, underground speakeasies, and hidden alleyways in Honolulu where illegal activities thrive.

Unlocking Hidden Areas

- **Treasure Maps:** Found throughout the game world, these maps offer cryptic clues leading to secret locations.
- **Climbing and Parkour:** Some hidden areas are accessible only by **scaling cliffs, swinging on ropes, or performing acrobatic jumps**.
- **Environmental Clues:** Pay attention to **strange markings, unusual rock formations, or NPC rumors** to uncover secrets.

4.3 Environmental Interactions and Climbing Mechanics

Exploration in *Like a Dragon: Pirate Yakuza in Hawaii* isn't limited to walking and sailing. The game introduces a robust **climbing system and environmental interaction mechanics**, allowing Majima to engage with the world like never before.

Climbing Mechanics

- **Free Climbing:** Majima can **scale cliffs, walls, and ship masts** using a simple yet fluid climbing system.
- **Grappling Hook:** Unlockable later in the game, the grappling hook allows Majima to swing across gaps, rappel down cliffs, and even **pull enemies off ledges** during combat.

- **Dynamic Climbing Challenges:** Some areas feature **environmental hazards** like crumbling ledges, falling rocks, or slippery surfaces that require quick reflexes.

Environmental Interactions

- **Interactive Objects:** Barrels, crates, chandeliers, and more can be used in both combat and exploration.
  - **Example:** Cutting a rope to drop a crate on enemies or swinging from a chandelier to reach a high platform.
- **Destructible Environments:** Certain structures can be **broken during fights**, revealing hidden paths or loot.
- **Water Mechanics:** Majima can **swim, dive, and even fight in shallow waters**, adding verticality to aquatic environments.

Environmental Puzzles

- **Lever & Pulley Systems:** Common in pirate ruins and shipwrecks, requiring players to manipulate objects to open doors or activate mechanisms.
- **Light Reflection Puzzles:** Using mirrors or reflective surfaces to solve **ancient temple riddles**.
- **Pressure Plates:** Step on specific tiles in the correct order to unlock secret chambers.

4.4 Dynamic Weather and Day-Night Cycle Effects

The game world feels alive thanks to its **dynamic weather system** and a realistic **day-night cycle** that affects not just visuals, but gameplay mechanics, enemy behavior, and mission availability.

Dynamic Weather System

- **Tropical Storms:** Sudden rainstorms reduce visibility, create slippery surfaces, and trigger **rough seas** during naval battles.
  - **Gameplay Impact:** Sailing becomes more challenging, with ships rocking violently. On land, stealth is easier due to reduced enemy sightlines.
- **Foggy Mornings:** Thick fog adds an eerie atmosphere, perfect for ambushes or stealth missions.
- **Volcanic Ash Clouds:** Near volcanic islands, ashfall reduces stamina regeneration and causes minor environmental damage over time.
- **Tsunamis (Special Events):** Rare but catastrophic events where Majima must **escape rising floodwaters**, leading to thrilling set-piece sequences.

Day-Night Cycle Effects

- **Enemy Behavior:**
  - **Day:** More naval patrols, active marketplaces, and visible security forces.
  - **Night:** Gangs become bolder, with **illegal street fights** and **black-market deals** in full swing. Certain quests are only available after dark.
- **Mission Variations:** Some story missions change based on the time of day, offering different enemy placements or dialogue options.
- **Stealth Advantage:** Darkness makes it easier to avoid detection, adding tactical depth to infiltration missions.
- **NPC Schedules:** Townsfolk follow daily routines— **merchants open shops during the day**, while **drunk sailors and informants** populate taverns at night.

Weather-Dependent Missions and Events

- **Storm Heist Missions:** Certain side quests trigger only during specific weather conditions, like **robbing a ship under the cover of a storm**.
- **Hidden Caves Revealed:** Low tides during particular times of day can expose **secret caves** or sunken treasures.
- **Random World Events:** Dynamic encounters, such as **helping shipwreck survivors during a hurricane** or **fighting cursed pirates under a blood moon**.

Chapter 5: Naval Combat and Ship Customization

5.1 The Goromaru: Your Pirate Vessel

In *Like a Dragon: Pirate Yakuza in Hawaii*, your journey across the Pacific isn't complete without your trusty ship, **The Goromaru**. Named after Goro Majima himself, this vessel is more than just transportation—it's a **floating fortress, a mobile base, and a symbol of Majima's chaotic reign on the high seas.**

Design and Aesthetics

- **Unique Look:** The Goromaru blends traditional Japanese pirate ship architecture with rugged Yakuza flair—**ornate dragon carvings, crimson sails, and battle-worn hulls.**
- **Personalization:** Players can **customize the ship's colors, figurehead, flags, and even graffiti** to reflect Majima's wild personality.
- **Interior Spaces:** Unlike typical pirate games, you can explore the interior, including:
    - **Captain's Quarters:** Where Majima stores personal items, maps, and mementos from side quests.
    - **Crew Lounge:** Interact with your crew for mini-games, dialogue options, and bonding events.
    - **Armory:** A stash for ship weapon upgrades and rare collectibles.

Ship Functions

- **Mobile Hideout:** Fast travel, side mission planning, and crew management are all accessed from the Goromaru.
- **Combat Platform:** It's equipped with cannons, harpoons, and special Yakuza-inspired weaponry for **real-time naval battles**.
- **Treasure Storage:** A secure vault for looted treasure, rare materials, and contraband collected during raids.

5.2 Real-Time Naval Battles Explained

Naval combat in the game isn't just about blasting cannons. It's an intense, fast-paced experience that combines **strategic maneuvering, real-time action, and Yakuza-style chaos**.

Basic Controls and Mechanics

- **Ship Movement:** Control speed, direction, and positioning using a dynamic sailing system that factors in wind direction, ocean currents, and ship weight.
- **Cannon Fire:** Use **broadside cannons** for wide attacks or **precision harpoons** for targeted strikes. Aim manually for critical hits on enemy ships.
- **Boarding Actions:** Once an enemy ship is weakened, Majima can **leap onto enemy decks for close-quarters combat**—turning naval battles into brutal melee brawls.

Types of Naval Weapons

- **Standard Cannons:** Reliable for long-range attacks, with upgrade options for increased damage.

- **Flame Throwers:** Mounted flamethrowers for **close-range devastation**, perfect for setting enemy decks ablaze.
- **Chain Shot:** Specialized cannonballs designed to **cripple enemy masts**, slowing down faster ships.
- **Explosive Kegs:** Throwable from the deck or launched via catapults—these kegs explode on impact, causing **massive area damage**.

Special Combat Features

- **Adrenaline Mode:** Similar to Majima's "Mad Dog" fighting style, the ship can enter a rage-like state where damage output increases temporarily, and the crew fights more aggressively.
- **Environmental Hazards:** Use the environment to your advantage—**navigate enemy ships into reefs, whirlpools, or explosive barrels** floating in the water.
- **Boss Battles:** Face off against **legendary sea creatures, enemy pirate lords, and even military warships** in multi-phase battles with cinematic flair.

5.3 Upgrading Your Ship: Weapons, Armor, and Crew

To survive the treacherous Pacific, the Goromaru needs constant upgrades. These enhancements not only improve performance but also add new tactical options during naval encounters.

Weapons Upgrades

- **Enhanced Cannons:** Improve firing speed, range, and damage.

- **Harpoon Launchers:** Essential for both combat and **hunting sea monsters**.
- **Deck-mounted Machine Guns:** A modern twist for rapid-fire attacks against smaller, fast-moving targets.

Armor and Defensive Modifications

- **Reinforced Hull:** Increases durability against cannon fire and ramming attacks.
- **Fireproof Coating:** Reduces damage from incendiary weapons.
- **Shockwave Plating:** An advanced upgrade that triggers a **defensive pulse** when the ship takes critical damage, pushing back nearby enemies.

Crew Management and Upgrades

- **Recruit Diverse Crew Members:** Each crew member has unique skills—some boost combat efficiency, while others enhance sailing speed or repair capabilities.
- **Crew Training:** Assign crew to specialized roles like **gunners, navigators, medics, or saboteurs**.
- **Bonding Events:** Strengthening relationships with crew members unlocks **special abilities and morale boosts** during battles.

Customization Options

- **Cosmetic Skins:** Unlock rare ship designs through story missions, side quests, or treasure hunts.
- **Figureheads with Buffs:** Some figureheads aren't just decorative—they grant passive bonuses like faster reload times or improved speed in storms.

- **Deck Decorations:** Customize with flags, banners, and even **neon Yakuza signs** for that signature Majima style.

5.4 Strategies for Sea Exploration and Naval Dominance

Conquering the seas isn't just about brute force. To establish Majima's dominance, you'll need a mix of **tactical thinking, resource management, and piracy expertise**.

Combat Strategies

- **Flanking Maneuvers:** Use speed and positioning to **attack enemy ships from their blind spots**, avoiding their strongest defenses.
- **Hit-and-Run Tactics:** Against larger ships, fire a quick barrage and retreat before they can retaliate.
- **Boarding Focus:** Sometimes, it's more profitable to **board and loot** an enemy ship rather than sinking it. This way, you collect more resources.
- **Environmental Warfare:** Lure enemies into dangerous waters—like near **volcanic islands** with lava flows or into **storm zones** where visibility is low.

Resource Management at Sea

- **Ammo & Supplies:** Cannonballs, food, and repair materials are limited. Make sure to **stock up at friendly ports** or loot from defeated ships.
- **Crew Morale:** Long voyages without victories or rest can cause crew morale to drop, affecting performance. Engage in **crew events** like feasts, songs, or storytelling to keep spirits high.

- **Weather Awareness:** Avoid sailing blindly into storms unless you're prepared. Use the ship's **weather tracking tools** to predict dangerous conditions.

Establishing Naval Dominance

- **Seizing Control Points:** Capture strategic ports and **pirate fortresses** to expand your influence. These locations generate income and provide safe havens.
- **Reputation System:** Your actions on the high seas affect your reputation. A feared pirate will be **hunted by naval forces** but respected by criminal factions.
- **Rival Pirate Captains:** Engage in epic duels with notorious pirate leaders. Defeating them not only brings loot but also **enhances your legend**, attracting stronger crew members.

Hidden Naval Secrets

- **Legendary Ship Hunts:** Track down **mythical ghost ships** and lost treasure fleets for rare loot.
- **Secret Sea Routes:** Discover hidden passages that allow for **faster travel** or access to uncharted islands.
- **Supernatural Events:** Occasionally, the sea behaves… strangely. Beware of **phantom fogs, cursed waters, and sea monsters** lurking where maps say nothing exists.

Chapter 6: Quests, Side Missions, and Story Progression

6.1 Main Story Missions Breakdown

The heart of *Like a Dragon: Pirate Yakuza in Hawaii* lies in its gripping main story missions, which follow **Goro Majima's wild odyssey** from notorious Yakuza to feared pirate legend. The story unfolds across multiple acts, each packed with cinematic sequences, high-stakes battles, and unexpected twists that showcase Majima's chaotic charm.

Story Structure

- **Acts & Chapters:** The narrative is divided into **5 Acts**, each with several chapters that escalate in intensity.
- **Mission Variety:** Expect a mix of **combat-heavy scenarios, stealth infiltrations, naval warfare, puzzle-solving, and emotional character moments**.
- **Cinematic Cutscenes:** True to the Yakuza series, the game features **beautifully directed cutscenes** with dynamic camera angles, dramatic voice acting, and occasional absurd humor.

Key Mission Types

1. **Assassination Contracts:** Take out high-profile targets using a mix of stealth and combat.

2. **Infiltration Missions:** Sneak into enemy fortresses, naval bases, or royal mansions, often with disguised identities.
3. **Naval Sieges:** Engage in large-scale sea battles, where you must **sink fleets or board flagship vessels**.
4. **Legendary Duels:** Face off against rival pirate lords and martial arts masters in epic one-on-one showdowns.
5. **Mythical Quests:** Some main missions delve into **supernatural elements**, like cursed relics or sea monsters tied to Hawaiian legends.

Memorable Story Missions

- **"The Mad Dog Sets Sail"** – Majima's chaotic introduction to piracy, featuring a bar fight that escalates into a full naval chase.
- **"Whispers of Madlantis"** – An underwater heist inside a sunken city filled with ancient traps and ghostly foes.
- **"The Crimson Mutiny"** – A betrayal within Majima's crew leads to an intense battle aboard the Goromaru itself.
- **"Dance of the Dragon's Fang"** – A climactic duel against a legendary pirate lord atop a burning ship during a thunderstorm.

6.2 Side Quests: Hidden Stories and Rewards

Side quests, known as **"Substories"**, are where the game's signature charm shines. These missions range from **hilarious encounters with quirky NPCs to deeply emotional narratives** that flesh out the world and characters.

Types of Side Quests

1. **Character-Driven Stories:**
   - Help crew members resolve personal conflicts or discover hidden backstories.
   - Example: **"The Cook's Secret Recipe"**—assist your ship's chef in finding rare ingredients, only to discover he's hiding a darker past.
2. **Bizarre and Absurd Adventures:**
   - Expect Majima to get involved in **comically ridiculous situations**.
   - Example: **"The Chicken Who Ruled the Seas"**—a quest where Majima befriends a pirate crew led by an actual chicken.
3. **Treasure Hunts and Lost Relics:**
   - Solve riddles and follow maps to uncover **hidden treasures, legendary weapons, or cursed artifacts**.
   - Example: **"The Curse of the Golden Coconut"**—a treasure hunt that turns into a supernatural survival mission.
4. **Combat Challenges:**
   - Enter illegal fighting tournaments, duel rogue samurai, or participate in naval battle arenas for rare loot.
5. **Favors for NPCs:**
   - Help villagers, merchants, and pirates with odd jobs like **finding lost items, protecting cargo, or even matchmaking**.

Rewards for Completing Side Quests

- **Unique Weapons & Gear:** Some of the most powerful items are locked behind side missions.

- **Crew Members:** Certain quests allow you to **recruit special crew members** with unique abilities.
- **Money & Resources:** Gain valuable loot to upgrade your ship and equipment.
- **Unlocking Hidden Areas:** Some quests reveal **secret islands, dungeons, or naval routes**.
- **Stat Boosts:** Completing specific challenges can **permanently enhance Majima's abilities**.

6.3 Managing Quest Logs and Objectives

With countless main missions, side quests, and activities, *Like a Dragon: Pirate Yakuza in Hawaii* provides a **robust quest management system** to help you stay organized.

Quest Log Interface

- **Categories:** Quests are sorted into tabs—**Main Story, Substories, Bounty Hunts, and Crew Missions**.
- **Priority Markers:** Color-coded icons distinguish between critical missions, side activities, and time-sensitive quests.
- **Detailed Objectives:** Each quest includes a clear list of objectives, current progress, and NPC locations.

Tracking & Navigation

- **Active Quest Tracking:** Set an active quest to display **waypoints and markers** on your map.
- **Dynamic Map Integration:** As you explore, new quests **automatically appear** on the map when you overhear rumors or interact with NPCs.

- **Quest Reminders:** Periodic notifications remind you of **unfinished quests** or alert you when conditions are met to continue.

Managing Complex Missions

- **Multi-Stage Quests:** Some storylines unfold over time. For example, a crew member's personal quest might only progress after completing key main missions.
- **Branching Paths:** Choice-based quests update dynamically based on your decisions. If an NPC dies due to your actions, their questline ends permanently.
- **Failed Objectives:** If you fail certain conditions, the game **offers alternative outcomes** rather than forcing a restart.

6.4 Choice-Driven Outcomes and Multiple Endings

Unlike previous Yakuza titles, *Pirate Yakuza in Hawaii* introduces a **choice-driven narrative** with **multiple endings** shaped by your actions throughout the game.

Key Decision Points

- **Major Choices:**
  - Decide the fate of key characters—**spare an enemy captain for alliances or execute them for fear-based dominance**.
  - Choose between loyalty to your crew or personal ambitions, affecting relationships and mission outcomes.
- **Moral Dilemmas:**

- Quests often present **gray moral choices**, where neither option is clearly right or wrong.
- Example: Do you betray an ally for strategic gain or uphold your honor, risking your crew's safety?

How Choices Impact the World

- **Crew Loyalty:** Your decisions influence crew morale. Betray them too often, and **mutiny becomes a real threat**.
- **Faction Relationships:** Align with pirate factions, rebel groups, or even colonial forces. Each choice **affects side quests, trade opportunities, and allies** available.
- **Dynamic Dialogue:** NPCs react differently based on your past actions—**some fear you, others respect you, and a few might seek revenge**.

Multiple Endings Explained

The game features **three primary endings**, with numerous variations based on side quests completed, crew relationships, and key story decisions.

1. **The Pirate King Ending:**
   - Majima becomes the undisputed ruler of the Pacific, feared by all. This path involves **ruthless choices, betrayals, and a high body count**.
2. **The Legend of the Seas Ending:**
   - Majima forges lasting alliances, leading a united pirate fleet while maintaining strong personal bonds. A more **balanced, diplomatic approach** unlocks this outcome.
3. **The Lone Wolf Ending:**

- A tragic, solitary ending where Majima sacrifices everything for vengeance, power, or personal obsession, depending on player choices.

Secret Ending:

- **"The Mad Dog's Requiem":** A hidden, bittersweet ending unlocked only by completing **100% of side quests, achieving max crew loyalty, and uncovering all hidden relics**. It reveals a surprising twist tied to Majima's past and the Yakuza legacy.

Chapter 7: Mini-Games and Activities

7.1 Karaoke, Dragon Kart, and Crazy Delivery

Mini-games are a staple of the *Like a Dragon* series, and *Pirate Yakuza in Hawaii* takes them to the next level by blending classic Yakuza charm with a tropical pirate twist. Whether you're looking for high-octane thrills, absurd fun, or rhythm-based challenges, this chapter covers all the must-try activities.

Karaoke: Majima's Musical Mayhem

- **How It Works:** Karaoke returns with an over-the-top, rhythm-based mini-game where players hit timed button prompts to keep the beat.
- **Song Selection:** Expect a mix of **traditional Yakuza hits, new pirate-themed tracks, and Hawaiian-inspired tunes**.
  - **Majima's Signature Song:** *"Mad Dog of the High Seas"*—a chaotic rock anthem with hilarious cutscenes showing Majima's wild imagination.
- **Duets & Crew Karaoke:** For the first time, you can **sing duets with crew members**, unlocking unique interactions and friendship bonuses.
- **Visuals:** The background transforms into Majima's bizarre fantasies—imagine him **surfing on a giant octopus while shredding an electric shamisen**.

Dragon Kart: Tropical Drift Showdown

- **Overview:** A spinoff of *Yakuza's Dragon Kart*, this pirate-themed racing game lets you race **customizable go-karts** across the islands of Hawaii.
- **Tracks:**
  - **Volcano Drift:** Navigate molten lava hazards.
  - **Beach Blitz:** Race along sandy shores, dodging waves and beachgoers.
  - **Jungle Jam:** A dense, twisty track with hidden shortcuts through waterfalls.
- **Weapons & Power-Ups:**
  - **Coconut Bombs:** Explode on impact.
  - **Harpoon Boost:** A speed boost with a chance to knock out opponents.
  - **Kraken Ink:** Temporarily blinds rival racers' screens.
- **Customization:** Upgrade your kart's speed, handling, and aesthetics. You can even slap a **Majima eye-patch decal** on your ride.
- **Multiplayer:** Compete against NPCs or friends in split-screen mode.

Crazy Delivery: Pirate Edition

Inspired by *Crazy Taxi*, this fast-paced delivery game sees Majima (or crew members) taking on the role of a **chaotic pirate courier**.

- **Objective:** Deliver bizarre items—like a crate of parrots, barrels of rum, or a suspiciously large "cursed treasure"—within a time limit.
- **Gameplay:**
  - **High-Speed Maneuvers:** Perform **drift turns, flips, and stunts** to reach destinations faster.

- o **Obstacles:** Dodge rival pirates, wild animals, and even random NPCs causing havoc.
- o **Over-the-Top Reactions:** Customers react hilariously based on your delivery style, ranging from grateful cheers to **full-blown chases if you damage their goods**.
- **Rewards:** Earn money, reputation points, and unlock special delivery routes with higher difficulty.

7.2 Classic Sega 8-Bit Games

As with previous Yakuza titles, *Pirate Yakuza in Hawaii* features fully playable **classic Sega 8-bit arcade games**, offering a nostalgic break from the main story.

Arcade Locations

- Found in **underground gambling dens, pirate hideouts, and shady bars** across the islands.
- Each arcade machine costs in-game currency to play, but **winning streaks reward rare items** or collectible tokens.

Featured Sega Games

1. **OutRun: Tropical Fury Edition**
   - o A special version with new tracks inspired by the Hawaiian setting.
2. **Space Harrier**
   - o Classic rail shooter with a pirate-themed reskin— fight flying ships and sea monsters instead of aliens.
3. **Fantasy Zone**
   - o A colorful shoot-'em-up where you control a pirate ship instead of the original spaceship.

4. **Super Hang-On**
   - Motorcycle racing with Majima-themed skins and custom bikes.

Hidden Arcade Challenges

- **High Score Competitions:** Compete against NPCs' high scores for bonus rewards.
- **Secret Unlockables:** Achieving top scores unlocks **rare cosmetics, crew recruitment opportunities, or even hidden quests**.
- **Majima's Commentary:** While playing, Majima occasionally **breaks the fourth wall**, making snarky remarks about the games.

7.3 Gambling Dens, Fishing, and Bar Challenges

The world of *Pirate Yakuza in Hawaii* is filled with activities beyond fighting and quests. Whether you prefer testing your luck, relaxing with a fishing rod, or competing in drinking contests, there's something for every playstyle.

Gambling Dens: Luck of the Mad Dog

- **Locations:** Hidden in **pirate coves, underground taverns, and back-alley speakeasies**.
- **Games Available:**
  1. **Poker:** High-stakes pirate poker with unique "all-in" animations.
  2. **Blackjack:** Featuring eccentric pirate dealers who **taunt or cheer** depending on your luck.

3. **Cho-Han:** Traditional Japanese dice game with tense betting rounds.
4. **Mahjong:** A full-fledged mini-game with complex strategies for veteran players.

- **Unique Twist:** Some dens offer **"cheating mechanics"**, allowing you to bribe dealers or sneak peeks at cards—**but getting caught leads to brawls.**

Fishing: Ocean Bounty

- **Mechanics:** A detailed fishing mini-game where players cast their lines into rivers, lakes, and the open sea.
- **Fishing Gear:** Upgrade rods, bait, and lures to catch **rare fish, treasure chests, and even bizarre sea creatures.**
- **Legendary Fish:**
  - **The Kraken Carp:** A mythical fish said to capsize small boats.
  - **Golden Tuna:** Worth a fortune if sold but can be displayed as a trophy on the Goromaru.
- **Interactive Combat:** When reeling in massive catches, Majima engages in **quick-time events** to avoid being dragged into the water—sometimes triggering **hilarious slapstick cutscenes.**

Bar Challenges: Drink Like a Pirate

- **Drinking Contests:** Compete against NPCs in **sake chugging competitions**, rum shots, and exotic Hawaiian cocktails.
- **Unique Mechanics:**
  - **Stamina Bar:** Manage your tolerance by timing sips carefully.

- o **Drunk Effects:** Winning or losing affects Majima's status—**temporary buffs in combat** or hilarious drunken debuffs like wobbling movements.
- **Bartender Quests:** Build relationships with bartenders to unlock **special drinks with stat-boosting effects**.

7.4 Earning Rewards Through Mini-Games

While mini-games are fun on their own, they also offer tangible rewards that can enhance your gameplay experience.

Types of Rewards

1. **In-Game Currency:**
   - o Winning gambling games, races, or high-stakes challenges earns **large sums of money** to spend on gear, upgrades, or luxury items.
2. **Equipment & Items:**
   - o **Rare Weapons:** Win fighting tournaments to unlock unique swords, like the **"Flaming Katana of the Pacific."**
   - o **Cosmetics:** Customize Majima's outfits, the Goromaru's appearance, or crew uniforms.
   - o **Boost Items:** Earn health potions, stamina boosts, and temporary combat buffs.
3. **Crew Members:**
   - o Certain mini-games allow you to **recruit new crew members** with special abilities.
   - o Example: Winning a drinking contest against a retired pirate captain might convince them to join your crew.

4. **Secret Unlockables:**
   ○ **Hidden Side Quests:** Some mini-games trigger secret questlines. For instance, achieving a perfect score in karaoke might unlock a **musical showdown side quest**.
   ○ **Legendary Titles:** Earn **titles and achievements** displayed in your player profile, boosting reputation in-game.

Mini-Game Mastery System

- **Progress Tracker:** The game features a **"Mini-Game Mastery Log"** that tracks your progress in each activity.
- **Rank System:** Achieve ranks like **Bronze, Silver, Gold, and Platinum** based on performance.
- **Mastery Bonuses:** Reaching the highest rank in all mini-games unlocks the **"Mad Dog of Leisure" title**, along with powerful gameplay bonuses.

Synergy with Main Gameplay

- **Combat Buffs:** Some mini-games provide **permanent stat boosts**—winning enough Dragon Kart races might improve Majima's sprint speed on foot.
- **Story Tie-Ins:** Certain side quests require completing mini-games to advance the plot or unlock new character interactions.
- **Bonding Opportunities:** Play mini-games with crew members to **strengthen relationships**, unlocking new abilities and dialogue options.

Chapter 8: Crew Management and Recruitment

8.1 How to Recruit Pirates and Specialists

Recruiting the right crew is vital to Majima's rise as a pirate legend in *Like a Dragon: Pirate Yakuza in Hawaii.* Your crew isn't just a group of background characters—they're **key allies who impact combat, navigation, and story progression**.

Where to Find Crew Members

- **Story Missions:** Some characters join automatically through the main story, often after dramatic encounters or battles.
- **Side Quests (Substories):** Completing side missions may unlock unique crew members with special skills.
- **Taverns and Pirate Dens:** Talk to NPCs in **pirate hideouts, seedy bars, and remote islands**. Impress them with feats of strength, gambling wins, or favors.
- **Bounty Hunts:** Defeated rivals can sometimes be recruited instead of eliminated—if you offer the right deal.

Recruitment Requirements

1. **Reputation Level:** Some specialists require Majima to have a high enough reputation as a pirate. Completing quests, winning battles, and making impactful choices boost this.
2. **Bribery or Persuasion:** Certain NPCs can be recruited through **bribes, gifts, or persuasive dialogue options**.

3. **Dueling for Loyalty:** Some tough characters demand a **one-on-one duel** with Majima before they'll respect him enough to join.
4. **Moral Alignment:** Your choices in the game affect recruitment. For example, ruthless characters may only join if Majima has a fearsome reputation, while others prefer a more honorable leader.

Notable Recruitable Crew Members

- **Reiko the Red-Eyed Sharpshooter:** A sniper found in a Hawaiian village, recruited after helping her defeat bounty hunters.
- **"Big Tuna" Makoto:** A former sumo wrestler turned pirate cook with combat buffs tied to food-based skills.
- **Captain Lono:** A disgraced naval officer who offers advanced navigation abilities after you save him from execution.
- **Kiko the Trickster:** A street magician specializing in distraction tactics during battles.

8.2 Crew Roles: Combat, Navigation, and Support

Your crew isn't just for show—they each serve specific roles that impact both **ship performance** and **combat scenarios**. Assigning the right person to the right job can mean the difference between victory and defeat.

Core Crew Roles

1. **Combat Specialists:**

- o **Role:** Join Majima in battle, providing direct support with unique abilities.
- o **Abilities:**
  - **Brawlers:** Heavy damage dealers with high HP.
  - **Sharpshooters:** Ranged attackers using pistols, rifles, or even thrown explosives.
  - **Tacticians:** Buff allies or debuff enemies with status effects.
- o **Combat Synergy:** Some crew combos trigger **"Team Attacks"**—special moves with cinematic finishers.

2. **Navigation Officers:**
   - o **Role:** Improve the Goromaru's performance at sea.
   - o **Skills:**
     - **Helmsmen:** Boost ship speed and maneuverability.
     - **Navigators:** Reveal hidden routes, avoid storms, and reduce travel time.
     - **Cartographers:** Add secret locations to the world map.

3. **Support Crew:**
   - o **Role:** Enhance out-of-combat activities like crafting, trading, and healing.
   - o **Specialists:**
     - **Cooks:** Prepare meals that grant temporary combat buffs.
     - **Blacksmiths:** Upgrade weapons and repair ship damage faster.
     - **Medics:** Heal Majima and other crew members after tough battles.

4. **Morale Officers:**
   - o **Role:** Keep the crew's spirits high to avoid conflicts and boost efficiency.

- Unique Skills: Some characters have **charisma bonuses** that improve overall crew loyalty or reduce the risk of mutiny.

Crew Management Interface

- **Crew Roster:** Displays all recruited members with stats, roles, and loyalty levels.
- **Assignment Screen:** Easily swap crew between active roles on the ship or in combat squads.
- **Skill Trees:** Some crew members have **individual skill trees** you can invest in to unlock new abilities or passive bonuses.

8.3 Building Loyalty and Crew Morale

A strong crew is more than just numbers—it's about loyalty. The happier and more loyal your crew, the more effective they'll be in both combat and daily ship operations.

Loyalty System Overview

- **Loyalty Levels:** Measured in **5 tiers**, from *Suspicious* to *Devoted*.
- **Benefits of High Loyalty:**
    - **Combat Buffs:** Crew fight harder for a leader they respect, gaining attack or defense bonuses.
    - **Special Skills:** Some abilities are unlocked only when loyalty reaches a certain level.
    - **Mutiny Prevention:** High loyalty reduces the chance of crew conflicts or betrayal.

How to Build Loyalty

1. **Complete Personal Quests:** Many crew members have **character-specific missions**. Helping them with personal problems increases their loyalty.
2. **Share Meals:** Organize **crew dinners** using ingredients from your travels. These casual interactions deepen bonds and reveal hidden backstories.
3. **Praise and Recognition:** After battles, Majima can **praise standout crew members**, giving a small loyalty boost.
4. **Decision-Making:** Making choices aligned with a crew member's values improves loyalty. For example, sparing an enemy might impress a compassionate crew member but upset a ruthless one.
5. **Gift System:** Certain crew members respond positively to specific gifts found or purchased during your journey.

Crew Bond Events

Unlock special **"Bond Events"**—short, often humorous or heartfelt scenes that reveal more about each crew member's personality. These events often lead to loyalty boosts or even new abilities.

8.4 Managing Crew Conflicts and Mutinies

A pirate crew isn't always smooth sailing. **Conflicts, rivalries, and even mutinies** can arise if loyalty drops too low or if crew members have clashing personalities.

Crew Conflicts

- **Causes:**

1. **Mismatched Values:** Pairing crew members with opposite moral codes in the same squad can create tension.
2. **Unresolved Grudges:** Some recruits have **pre-existing rivalries** that escalate if not addressed.
3. **Leadership Decisions:** Ruthless or reckless decisions might demoralize certain crew members.
- **How to Manage Conflicts:**
  1. **Mediation:** Hold a **crew meeting** to address grievances. Majima can choose dialogue options to defuse tension or side with one party.
  2. **One-on-One Talks:** Engage in private conversations to understand and resolve personal issues.
  3. **Reassign Roles:** Separating feuding crew members reduces the chance of fights breaking out.

Mutiny Mechanics

If morale drops too low across the ship, it can trigger a **mutiny event**, forcing Majima to confront the consequences.

- **Warning Signs:**
  1. Decreased performance in ship duties.
  2. Passive-aggressive comments from crew.
  3. NPCs spreading rumors of discontent.
- **Mutiny Event Types:**
  1. **Small-Scale Rebellion:** A fight breaks out between a few disgruntled crew members. Majima must intervene before it escalates.
  2. **Full Mutiny:** If ignored, the situation can lead to an all-out mutiny, where Majima must **fight his own crew** to regain control.

Consequences of Mutiny:

- **Permanent Death:** Some crew members may be killed during a mutiny, affecting the story and gameplay permanently.
- **Loss of Resources:** A successful mutiny can result in stolen supplies, damaged equipment, or even loss of the ship (requiring a retrieval mission).
- **Rebuilding Trust:** Surviving a mutiny reduces the loyalty of the entire crew, forcing Majima to **rebuild morale** through quests and interactions.

Preventing Mutiny:

- **Regular Morale Checks:** Organize events like celebrations after big victories.
- **Balanced Leadership:** Mix **fear and respect**—sometimes ruthless decisions are needed to maintain order, but fairness fosters long-term loyalty.
- **Legendary Status:** If Majima reaches a certain reputation level, his **fearsome legend alone** can suppress dissent.

Chapter 9: Combat Strategies and Boss Fights

9.1 Basic Combat Tactics for Beginners

For newcomers to the *Like a Dragon* series or those adjusting to the new pirate-themed setting, understanding the fundamentals of combat is key. The game blends **brawler-style melee combat** with dynamic environmental interactions, creating a system that's both accessible and deep.

Understanding Combat Basics

- **Controls Overview:**
    - **Light Attack (Quick Combos):** Great for building combos and staggering enemies.
    - **Heavy Attack (Power Strikes):** Slower but deals more damage and can break enemy guards.
    - **Guard/Block:** Reduces incoming damage; timing it perfectly can trigger a **parry**.
    - **Dodge (Roll/Quick Step):** Essential for avoiding powerful attacks, especially against bosses.
- **Target Lock System:**
  Lock onto enemies to focus your attacks, making it easier to dodge and counter specific threats.
- **Stamina and Resource Bars:**
    - **Stamina:** Governs how many actions you can perform in quick succession.
    - **Heat Gauge:** Builds as you deal damage, allowing you to unleash devastating **Heat Actions—**

cinematic finishers unique to each weapon or scenario.

Combat Flow:

1. **Engage with Light Attacks:** Start combos to keep enemies off balance.
2. **Mix in Heavy Strikes:** Break guards or launch enemies into the air.
3. **Utilize Dodging:** Avoid counterattacks, especially from stronger foes.
4. **Environmental Finishes:** Grab objects (like barrels, crates, or even oars) to perform brutal environmental takedowns.

Beginner Tips:

- **Don't Button Mash:** The combat system rewards timing and precision.
- **Learn Enemy Patterns:** Even basic enemies have tells before strong attacks.
- **Use the Environment:** Weapons and interactive objects are scattered throughout combat zones—don't ignore them.
- **Manage Resources:** Save your Heat Gauge for tough situations like boss fights.

9.2 Advanced Techniques for Veteran Players

For experienced players seeking to master the combat system, *Pirate Yakuza in Hawaii* offers a wealth of advanced mechanics. Mastery involves not just surviving but dominating every encounter with style and efficiency.

Perfect Dodge and Counter Mechanics

- **Perfect Dodge:** Executed by dodging at the exact moment an enemy attack lands. Grants brief invincibility and leaves the attacker vulnerable.
- **Counter Strikes:** After a perfect dodge, you can follow up with a **powerful counterattack** that deals bonus damage.
- **Parry Timing:** Perfectly timed blocks reflect damage back at the attacker or stagger them for an easy follow-up.

Style Switching Mid-Combat

- **Mad Dog vs. Sea Dog Styles:**
  - **Mad Dog Style:** Fast, aggressive, focused on overwhelming opponents with flurries of strikes.
  - **Sea Dog Style:** More defensive and strategic, incorporating grapples, disarms, and ranged attacks.
- **Combo Chaining:** Switch styles mid-combo for fluid, high-damage sequences. For example, start with Mad Dog for quick hits, then switch to Sea Dog for a grapple finisher.

Heat Actions and Environmental Kills

- **Advanced Heat Actions:**
  - **Weapon-Based:** Use swords, spears, or even makeshift weapons like broken bottles.
  - **Environmental:** Slam enemies into walls, overboard (during ship fights), or into explosive barrels for massive area damage.
  - **Team Heat Actions:** Trigger **special team attacks** with crew members, often with cinematic finishers.
- **Heat Action Timing:** Build your Heat Gauge strategically—don't waste it on weak enemies when a boss is approaching.

Crowd Control Strategies

- **Area of Effect (AoE) Attacks:** Certain heavy strikes and Heat Actions hit multiple enemies, ideal for crowd control.
- **Target Prioritization:**
  - Take out ranged attackers and healers first.
  - Stagger large groups with AoE, then isolate tougher enemies.
- **Throw Mechanics:** Grapple weaker enemies and **throw them into larger mobs** to knock down multiple foes at once.

Weapon Mastery and Combos

- **Weapon Durability:** Some weapons break after extended use, but high-level players can **maximize damage output** before that happens.
- **Combo Extensions:** Learn weapon-specific combo chains— **katanas have fast slashes**, while **heavy clubs deal slow, crushing blows**.
- **Hidden Techniques:** Certain rare weapons unlock **unique finisher moves** when used correctly.

9.3 Boss Battle Strategies and Weaknesses

Boss fights in *Pirate Yakuza in Hawaii* are epic, cinematic, and challenging. Each boss has unique mechanics, requiring tactical thinking beyond button-mashing.

Understanding Boss Patterns

- **Phases:** Most bosses have multiple phases, each with new attack patterns and abilities.
- **Tells:** Bosses telegraph their strongest moves. Watch for **glowing eyes, distinct sound cues, or exaggerated wind-ups**.
- **Weak Points:** Some bosses expose vulnerabilities during specific moves—capitalize on these windows for bonus damage.

Common Boss Archetypes & How to Counter Them

1. **The Bruiser (Tank-Type Bosses):**
   - **Example:** A giant pirate wielding a spiked anchor.
   - **Strategy:**
     - Dodge heavy swings.
     - Use fast attacks to chip away health.
     - Exploit their slow recovery after big moves.
2. **The Speed Demon (Agile Bosses):**
   - **Example:** A dual-dagger assassin who flips around the arena.
   - **Strategy:**
     - Use lock-on to maintain focus.
     - Parry quick attacks instead of trying to dodge everything.
     - Counter with grapples when they get close.
3. **The Trickster (Bosses with Gimmicks):**
   - **Example:** A pirate sorcerer who sets traps around the arena.
   - **Strategy:**
     - Destroy traps early to reduce battlefield hazards.

- Bait them into overextending before punishing with Heat Actions.
4. **The Naval Commander (Ship-Based Boss Fights):**
   - **Example:** A rival captain attacking from a fortified ship.
   - **Strategy:**
     - Use ship cannons strategically.
     - Board their ship to force close-quarters combat.
     - Manage crew abilities for support fire.

Boss Fight Survival Tips

- **Keep Healing Items Ready:** Always stock up before major story missions.
- **Crew Support:** In boss fights, crew members can offer buffs, distractions, or even join the fight directly.
- **Adapt:** If one strategy isn't working, switch combat styles or reposition to control the flow of battle.

9.4 Using Environment and Weapons to Your Advantage

One of the most thrilling aspects of *Like a Dragon: Pirate Yakuza in Hawaii* is the way you can manipulate the environment during combat. Whether you're fighting in narrow ship corridors or bustling Hawaiian streets, the surroundings are part of your arsenal.

Environmental Interactions

- **Destructible Objects:**
  - Break barrels, crates, or furniture to create improvised weapons.

- Explosive barrels can cause chain reactions when ignited.
- **Interactive Terrain:**
  - **Walls & Railings:** Slam enemies into hard surfaces for bonus damage. On ships, knock foes overboard to **instantly defeat** them.
  - **Ledges & Cliffs:** Trigger **environmental finishers** by throwing enemies off cliffs or into shark-infested waters.
- **Dynamic Weather Effects:**
  - **Rain:** Makes the ground slippery, affecting enemy footing (and yours).
  - **High Winds (Naval Battles):** Impact projectile accuracy but can be used to your advantage if timed correctly.

Weapon Variety and Mastery

- **Weapon Types:**
  - **Melee Weapons:** Swords, spears, clubs, and makeshift objects like oars.
  - **Ranged Weapons:** Pistols, rifles, and thrown items (bottles, knives).
  - **Heavy Weapons:** Cannons (in naval battles), harpoons, and explosive barrels.
- **Weapon-Based Heat Actions:**
  - Each weapon has unique finishing moves. For example:
    - **Katana:** Quick slashes ending in a dramatic finishing blow.
    - **Anchor:** Brutal swings that **crush multiple enemies at once**.
    - **Improvised Weapons:** Absurd and hilarious Heat Actions, like beating someone with a

giant fish or slamming them into a vending machine.

Crowd Control Using the Environment

- **Bottleneck Tactics:** Lure groups into narrow spaces to limit how many can attack at once.
- **Chain Reactions:** Use environmental hazards to create chain reactions—ignite an oil spill to burn multiple enemies.
- **Trap Setups:** Some areas have **pre-set traps** (falling nets, loose cargo, collapsing structures) that can be triggered during combat.

Chapter 10: Secrets, Easter Eggs, and Post-Game Content

10.1 Hidden Treasures and Collectibles

In *Like a Dragon: Pirate Yakuza in Hawaii*, the world is brimming with **hidden treasures** and **collectibles** that reward exploration, curiosity, and a keen eye for detail. From secret stashes buried beneath palm trees to rare artifacts tucked away in forgotten caves, there's always something waiting to be discovered.

Treasure Maps and Clues

- **Treasure Maps:** Scattered throughout the game world, these maps often feature cryptic drawings, riddles, or coordinates that hint at the location of hidden loot.
- **Clues and NPC Rumors:** Talking to NPCs in taverns, docks, and markets can reveal rumors about legendary pirate treasures or hidden vaults.

Types of Collectibles

1. **Buried Chests:** Use your **treasure compass** or follow subtle environmental clues like disturbed sand to locate them.
2. **Rare Artifacts:** Historical relics from ancient Hawaiian culture or pirate history, collectible for both story lore and valuable trade.
3. **Legendary Weapons:** Some of the most powerful weapons are hidden in hard-to-reach places, requiring both puzzle-solving and combat prowess to obtain.

4. **Secret Messages:** Hidden notes, letters, and journals that expand on the game's lore, often unlocking new side quests.

Environmental Puzzles

Certain treasures require solving environmental puzzles:

- Aligning ancient symbols carved into rocks.
- Navigating underground cave systems.
- Completing time-based parkour challenges.

Rewards for Collectibles

- **Cash and Gear:** Valuable loot that can be sold or used to upgrade Majima's equipment.
- **Hidden Heat Actions:** Some collectibles unlock unique Heat Moves tied to rare weapons.
- **Trophies/Achievements:** Completionists will find plenty of challenges tied to finding every hidden item.

10.2 Unlockable Costumes, Weapons, and Abilities

Customization is a big part of the *Like a Dragon* experience, and *Pirate Yakuza in Hawaii* takes it to the next level with unlockable **costumes**, **weapons**, and **abilities** that let you personalize Majima and your crew.

Unlockable Costumes

- **Pirate-Themed Outfits:** Classic pirate gear, including tricorn hats, eye patches, and flamboyant coats.

- **Yakuza Throwbacks:** Unlock Majima's iconic snake-skin jacket and other outfits from previous games.
- **Hawaiian Vibes:** Casual beachwear like aloha shirts, board shorts, and even ridiculous costumes like a **giant pineapple suit** for comedic effect.

How to Unlock:

- Completing specific side quests.
- Defeating secret bosses.
- Collecting all treasures in certain regions.

Unlockable Weapons

- **Legendary Blades:** Swords with unique designs and abilities, such as the **"Crimson Tide Katana"** that leaves enemies bleeding over time.
- **Improvised Weapons:** Wacky and unconventional weapons, like a **surfboard** or a **giant fish**, perfect for hilarious Heat Actions.
- **Mythical Artifacts:** Weapons tied to Hawaiian mythology, imbued with elemental effects like fire, lightning, or poison.

Acquisition Methods:

- Defeating rare mini-bosses.
- Solving hidden environmental puzzles.
- Participating in high-tier combat tournaments.

Unlockable Abilities

- **Advanced Heat Actions:** Cinematic finishers with over-the-top animations.

- **Crew Combo Moves:** Special team-based abilities that allow Majima to perform devastating combo attacks with crew members.
- **Passive Perks:** Bonuses like faster stamina regeneration, increased loot drops, or enhanced critical hit chances.

10.3 Secret Bosses and Ultimate Challenges

For players seeking the ultimate test of their skills, *Pirate Yakuza in Hawaii* features **secret bosses** and **ultimate challenges** hidden beyond the main story. These encounters are not just difficult—they're designed to push your mastery of combat mechanics to the limit.

Secret Bosses

1. **The Phantom Corsair:** A legendary pirate ghost said to haunt the waters near Madlantis.
   - **Tactics:** Uses teleportation and cursed attacks that drain stamina.
2. **Shark King of Nele Island:** A giant mutated shark that's part-boss, part-environmental hazard during an epic naval battle.
   - **Tactics:** Requires controlling your ship's cannons while avoiding its devastating breaches.
3. **Yakuza from the Past:** An old rival from Majima's past makes a surprise appearance, blending classic Yakuza fighting styles with new pirate-themed moves.
   - **Tactics:** A fast, aggressive melee fight with minimal room for error.

Ultimate Challenges

- **Colosseum Tournaments:** Gladiator-style arenas with wave-based combat against increasingly difficult foes.
- **Time Trials:** Defeat a set number of enemies or bosses within strict time limits.
- **No-Heal Runs:** Special dungeons where you can't use healing items, forcing reliance on skill and resource management.

Rewards for Beating Secret Bosses:

- **Exclusive Gear:** Weapons and armor unavailable anywhere else.
- **Unique Titles/Achievements:** Badges of honor for completing the toughest fights.
- **Lore Expansions:** Hidden cutscenes and story reveals that tie into both the pirate setting and Majima's Yakuza past.

10.4 Post-Game Content and New Game+ Mode

After completing the main story, *Like a Dragon: Pirate Yakuza in Hawaii* opens up a wealth of **post-game content** to keep the adventure alive. Whether you're a completionist or someone seeking new challenges, there's plenty to do beyond the credits.

Post-Game Exploration

- **Unlocked Regions:** New islands and secret coves that weren't accessible during the main story.
- **Elite Bounty Hunts:** Track down the most dangerous pirates on the high seas for massive rewards.

- **Hidden Side Quests:** New storylines that dive deeper into supporting characters' backstories.

New Game+ Mode

- **Carry Over Progress:** Bring your levels, abilities, weapons, and costumes into a new playthrough.
- **Increased Difficulty Options:** Enemies are stronger, more aggressive, and bosses gain new attack patterns.
- **Alternate Story Choices:** Explore different narrative outcomes by making new decisions during key moments.

Legacy Mode (Yakuza Nostalgia Feature):

- **Classic Gameplay Elements:** Optional mode that tweaks combat to resemble classic Yakuza games, with limited Heat Actions and more grounded brawling mechanics.
- **Cameo Appearances:** Surprise encounters with characters from past *Like a Dragon* titles, hidden as Easter eggs.

Completionist Goals:

- **100% Completion Checklist:** Track every collectible, side quest, Heat Action, and hidden boss.
- **Secret Ending:** Unlock a special epilogue cutscene for achieving full completion, revealing Majima's next adventure.